RUSSIA

Tracy Vonder Brink

TABLE OF CONTENTS

A Crabtree Seedlings Book

School-to-Home Support for Caregivers and Teachers

This book helps children grow by letting them practice reading. Here are a few guiding questions to help the reader with building his or her comprehension skills. Possible answers appear here in red.

Before Reading:

- What do I think this book is about?
    - *I think this book is about Russia.*
    - *I think this book is about ways of life in Russia.*
- What do I want to learn about this topic?
    - *I want to learn where Russia is.*
    - *I want to learn about the weather in Russia.*

During Reading:

- I wonder why...
    - *I wonder why the domes of St. Basil's Cathedral are shaped like onions.*
    - *I wonder why so many brown bears live in Russia.*
- What have I learned so far?
    - *I have learned that Russia is in Europe and Asia.*
    - *I have learned that Moscow is Russia's biggest city.*

After Reading:

- What details did I learn about this topic?
    - *I have learned that the Ural Mountains are the longest mountain range in Russia.*
    - *I have learned that Siberia is very cold.*
- Read the book again and look for the vocabulary words.
    - *I see the word* ***capital*** *on page 4, and the word* ***domes*** *on page 6. The other glossary words are on pages 22 and 23.*

Russia is a country.

It is in **Europe** and **Asia**.

Moscow is the **capital**.

It is Russia's biggest city.

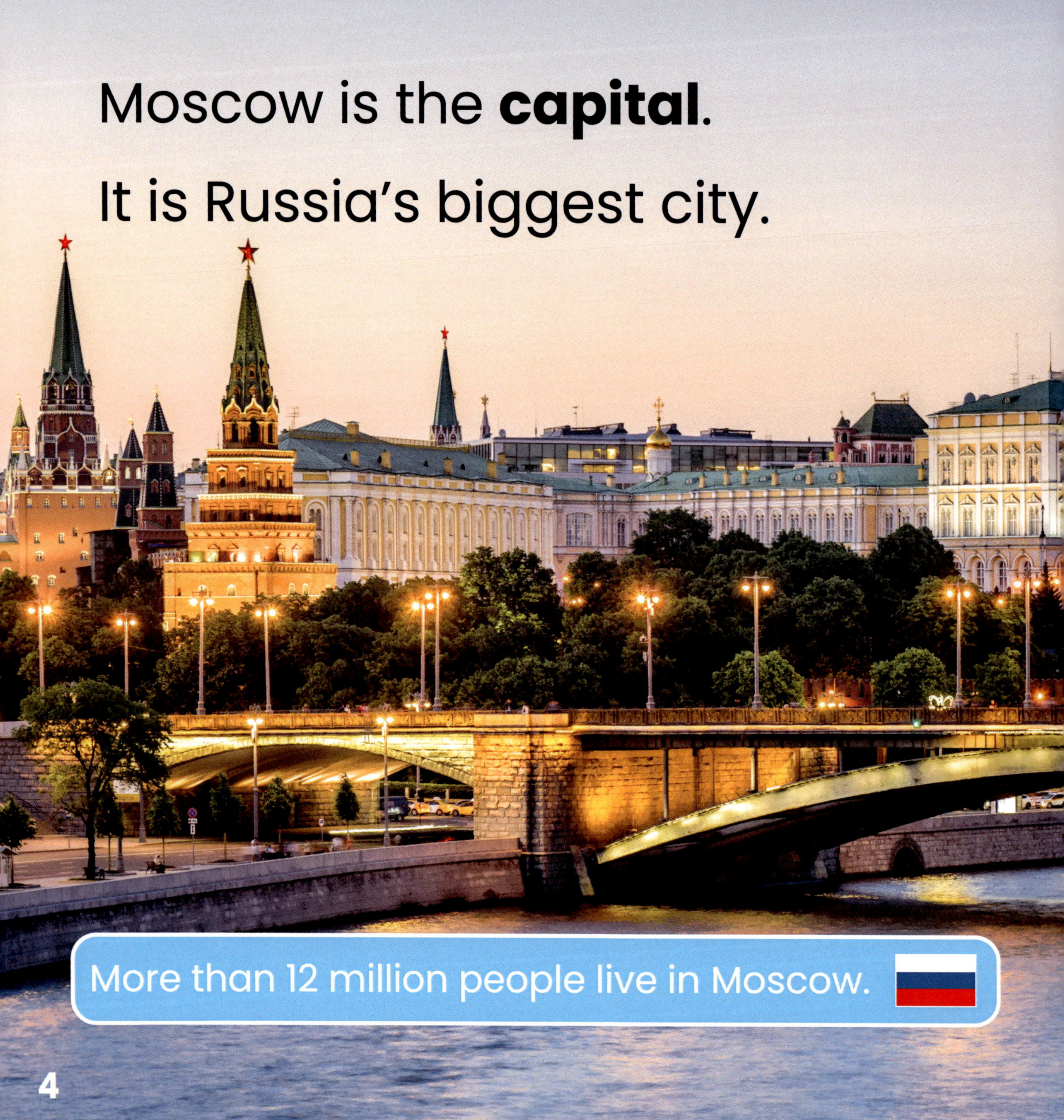

More than 12 million people live in Moscow.

Most people in Russia speak Russian.

St. Basil's Cathedral is a beautiful church in Moscow.

Its colorful **domes** are shaped like onions.

The Volga River flows through Moscow.

It also runs through several other large Russian cities.

The Volga is the longest river in Europe.

St. Petersburg is a **port** city.

It sits on the Baltic Sea.

The Eurasian **Steppe** stretches over much of Russia.

Saiga antelopes live there.

The Ural Mountains are the longest mountain range in Russia.

Brown bears make their homes in mountain forests.

Siberia is in northern Russia.

It is one of the coldest places in the world.

Much of Siberia is **taiga**.

Larch trees grow there.

Lake Baikal is in Siberia.

It is the oldest lake on Earth.

The East Siberian Sea is part of the Arctic Ocean.

Polar bears hunt on the ice.

Russia is a large country!

Glossary

Asia (AY-zhuh): The continent between Europe and Africa on one side and the Pacific Ocean on the other

capital (KAP-i-tl): The city where the government of a country or a state is located

domes (DOHMS): Rounded roofs or ceilings that are shaped like half a ball

Europe (YOOR-up): The continent between the Atlantic Ocean and Asia

port (PORT): A place where ships stop to load and unload cargo

steppe (STEP): A large area where the land is flat and grassy with few trees

taiga (TY-guh): An evergreen forest growing on swampy land in far northern regions

Index

About the Author

Tracy Vonder Brink

Tracy Vonder Brink loves to visit new places. She has never visited Russia, but she would like to see St. Basil's Cathedral. She lives in Cincinnati, Ohio, with her husband, two daughters, and two rescue dogs.

Written by: Tracy Vonder Brink
Designed by: Niko Magaro
Series Development: James Earley
Proofreader: Melissa Boyce
Educational Consultant: Marie Lemke M.Ed.

Photographs: All images from Shutterstock

Crabtree Publishing

crabtreebooks.com 800-387-7650

Printed in the U.S.A./062024/CG20240201

Published in Canada
Crabtree Publishing
616 Welland Avenue
St. Catharines, Ontario
L2M 5V6

Published in the United States
Crabtree Publishing
347 Fifth Avenue
Suite 1402-145
New York, New York, 10016

Library and Archives Canada Cataloguing in Publication
Available at Library and Archives Canada

Library of Congress Cataloging-in-Publication Data
Available at the Library of Congress

Hardcover: 978-1-0398-4483-4
Paperback: 978-1-0398-4564-0
Ebook (pdf): 978-1-0398-4636-4
Epub: 978-1-0398-4706-4
Read-Along: 978-1-0398-4776-7
Audio: 978-1-0398-4846-7